THE CORAL SEA

ALSO BY PATTI SMITH

Early Work: 1970–1979

THE CORAL SEA

PATTI SMITH

W. W. NORTON & COMPANY

NEW YORK · LONDON

For information about permission to reproduce selections from this book, write to Permissions, W. W. Norton & Company, Inc., 500 Fifth Avenue, New York, NY 10110.

The text of this book is composed in Adobe Caslon
with the display set in Charlemagne
Composition by Crane Typesetting Service, Inc.
Manufacturing by The Courier Companies, Inc.
Book design by Chris Welch

Library of Congress Cataloging-in-Publication Data
Smith, Patti.
      The coral sea / Patti Smith.
          p.   cm.
      ISBN 0-393-03908-0
      1. Mapplethorpe, Robert—Poetry.   2. Photographers—United States—
Poetry.   3. Photography—Poetry.   I. Title.
PS3569.M53787C67   1996
811′.54—dc20   95-38117

W. W. Norton & Company, Inc., 500 Fifth Avenue, New York, N.Y. 10110
W. W. Norton & Company Ltd., 10 Coptic Street, London WC1A 1PU

1   2   3   4   5   6   7   8   9   0

FOR ROBERT

Contents

TO THE READER

The first time I saw Robert he was sleeping. I stood over him, this boy of twenty, who sensing my presence opened his eyes and smiled. With few words he became my friend, my compeer, my beloved adventure.

When he became ill I wept and could not stop weeping. He scolded me for that, not with words but with a simple look of reproach, and I ceased.

When I saw him last we sat in silence and he rested his head on my shoulder. I watched the light changing over his hands, over his work, and over the whole of our lives. Later, returning to his bed, we said goodbye. But as I was leaving something stopped me and I went back to his room. He was sleeping. I stood over him, a dying man, who sensing my presence opened his eyes and smiled.

When he passed away I could not weep so I wrote. Then I took the pages and set them away. Here are those pages, my farewell to my friend, my adventure, my unfettered joy.

—

THE CORAL SEA

PROLOGUE

From a place apart, Morpheus, god of dreams, awakes. Detached from the benevolent folds of the muse he presses against the blue and burns into form. Flying high, with neither love nor remorse, he regards his charge—a young man asleep within the cloth of a voyage, which is turning, ever so slowly, even as the widening skirt of an ecstatic.

VOYAGE

THE PASSENGER M

The Passenger and those he leaves behind, connected for a moment by a long unwinding ribbon. A streamer cast and caught with joy. A ribbon of life snapping—pitched and tossed, wrapping round a wrist, gasping upon a wave or trampled upon below.

The Passenger is suddenly flattened. Perhaps it is the sight of wet crepe, a beloved port or a loved one fading—a tiny dot dissolving as the vast grainy sea takes over. Soon he is taken over as well by a sense of relief, of weightlessness, or by the courageous scent of his own volition.

The air is sweet. The arm of the sea curves and cradles, subduing all passion, and is a comfort and a lure.

The Passenger M is . . . musing . . .

Addressing perhaps . . . the void. The pit of the will which he pops like a stemless cherry. He regards his empty hand, the indifferent sea. If he were to step out upon that sea, would he be swallowed like an insect or supported like a king . . . Might he remove his slippers and walk upon the waves amongst the tiny fishes and draw from the swell a symphony of moans and hisses . . .

The sun appears from behind a rolling cloud. Sighing, the Passenger lets slide these notions for he is suddenly sleepy. With a nod to the elements he turns and makes his way to his cabin. The sun and sea, as a courtesy, commingle. The rays break and sparkle, lacquering the surface, as if in preparation for the perfect walk.

THE THROW

The sea was dense as a Rothko, prosaic, unbroken. But the shadows, they seemed to be everywhere; invading every hollow, every secret place, as a flapping of wings, where there were no birds, not even a gull.

Outside the stateroom, by the cabin door, a pair of dress boots stood guard. Within, a pair of custom shoes in their felt bags lay at the foot of the cot. A magnificent cot dressed in Egyptian linen. And upon it lay the sleeper, dreaming, beneath a faded throw.

It was a lovely thing, the throw, in an unusual shade of green. A burnished leaf forming its place among the threads of a protective vine. It had draped an old man's shoulders and something of him was pressed within its weathered folds.

On the bed stand objects meshed with the shifting light. A pack of *Gauloises Jaunes*, a ring carved from a single nugget and a small portrait, slightly blurred, in an oval frame. A youth in sailor garb, eyeing the world a bit suspiciously yet maintaining an air delicate as a lash, and possessing a manner at once smooth and brittle as a silk flag dipped in a pool and then left hanging on a thorn on a winter's night. This same young man was sleeping, en route to the Solomon Islands, dreaming of himself.

Of a boy who shuddered at every turn. Of a boy who constructed his own universe. Who reclaimed an altar within a tiny grotto. The walls were brushed a matte blue dotted with pale stars. His candle burned, revealing slim boxes of incense and, among the stones and burnt sticks, a small statue layered in dust. He wiped it with his sleeve and righted it. A swarm of half-formed prayers buzzed about his nodding head. How many times had he knelt praying to be somewhere, someone else. A rodeo star, a man straddling a mare or a motor bike with wings. He had prayed so hard he would rise from a pool of sweat, of feathers and a mouth full of flight.

On a summer's afternoon he would swim the brown river and regard with amazement the bright, turbulent sky. He would lie in the grass, upon the green blades, his green eyes closing as the sun drew him into sleep.

He was with Uncle and they were the only people in the world. He curled in Uncle's great lap, breathing very quietly as Uncle read from a worn copy of *Kim*, stopping here and there to recount an adventure of his own.

"One thing, I promise you, that you will never see in your own sky is the Southern Cross. That remarkable sign can only be seen by those who follow the skies of the Southern Hemisphere."

"Did you see it Uncle?"

"Yes, my boy, as a young man, and again, not long ago."

"Then I'll see it too Uncle. I'll see it as well."

"I believe you will, my boy. I believe you will."

And he nestled in the keep of the ship as he had nestled in the caring arms of his uncle. And the shadows, they seemed to be everywhere, playing upon him, defying the dress guard and casting silhouettes—a novice dancing, a thick rope swinging. And the shadows meshed and there was only night flapping; skimming the stillness outside the porthole.

And the cabin claimed him and the cabin was him. There was an aura of perfection even to the placement of objects. In the objects themselves. So that one, upon entering, would question nothing. Merely enter and find oneself lying upon the cot—austere, inviting, dressed in Egyptian linen—without knowing why.

Turning abruptly, M let drop a shoe which slipped from its felt bag at a right angle, landing on the gleaming floor in a ray of starlight, perfectly placed. He opened his eyes and closed them. For he was overcome with the warm sensation of being tucked in by unseen hands and covered tenderly with a soft green throw.

LIGHT PLAY

He was destined to be ill, quite ill, though it was not apparent. Youth alone would seem to account for his feverish spirit, the fever was becoming more and more demanding. The romantic garden within him raged with wild bloom, which he plucked and carelessly tossed in every direction. For he was no naturalist—more the archer, spraying arrows in a clearing suddenly sprouting statues. He had conjured a pedestal for his own amusement and he sat upon it and spun around. Art, not nature, moved him. Nature, he had boasted, was meant to be redesigned; opened and folded like a fan.

How those deer eyes peered above that fan and how often it was laid aside for the sake of refining an arrangement or the angle of a frame. He was born with a gift for placement, which he executed with the brash assurance of a young master. Adoring the prospect of a relationship not anticipated. The curve of a stem against the throat of a fallen goddess. A twist of net in an exposed hall. And, as one wandered into a space so deftly turned, one was really entering the miracle of a singular mind.

His delicate eyes saw with clarity what others did not. As a child, he arranged his toys with the order and ardor of a priest, and gave them properties that caused them to glow. He exasperated the manservant of a scholarly relation by revamping the entire library, compiling new harmonies whose notes were the colors and textures of the bindings. Endpapers, marbled petals of a flower of his own design, fanning an enormous Tabriz. He was scolded soundly, but it was not the scolding that made him cry but the disassembling of his handiwork. A rainbow of green Moroccan leather. He was led away weeping as the manservant, mumbling to himself, took on the task of placing the library in its former order.

And now a man, he adored a ruby flask but ignored its contents. He had ignored the cries of his own blood to linger over a particularly fine engraving or the feel of an exceptional sail.

He had ignored nature and now turned to her for his salvation, and set about to make peace with her, bowing to her mysteries. To beat the divinity, to set right destiny. His appointed lot would be overgrown with delicious vines which he would feast upon before he spun within a womb of silk.

He was venturing to Papua to secure for his soul a legendary butterfly, which he would tack to his chest as Pan had attached his shadow to his wild little feet. He would have those great wings embedded—stretched against his skin, over his shoulder blades, expanding over the heart that betrayed him by beating, wild, static; like little feet running in place.

The play of light upon the marble stairs and upon the trousers of an old gentleman descending. He became increasingly aware of light; just as he was also becoming aware of an impending black square drawing him in. Light masking the eyes of a coquette. Pencil rays striping his chest. He, a free man, to be

imprisoned in time by the whims of marble gods, themselves streaked with light. These reflections shot through the mind of one unaccustomed to reflection. Who was ruled by feelings, sensations. And anguish played in the pit of his being. That in his leave-taking so many things would be scattered like precious leaves upon the desert. Obtain a new place not placed by his hand.

He looked at his hand. How it trembled. Yet the heat was unbearable. No it was actually quite cool. In his heartlessness he had ignored nature, and how heartless nature was in return. To wreak havoc upon a soul so cunning as to presume to redesign the manner in which it would be eternally expelled from his trembling frame.

The process was underway, had begun earlier, upon the bridge, in full sun. He was extending the perimeters of his garden and with a gesture conceived a stag—erect, majestic. Gazing into the deer eyes of his creator—a youth upon the bridge.

He regarded, with irony, his feverish wand. Vegetation papered his cabin—a tomb of moss and fern. Great fish leapt and became trophies in his hand and the stag advanced and licked his palm.

How should I be charged, he whispered. For want of so much bounty. For rearranging eyes. For being one who wished nothing less than to embrace the spine of a mountain as the light played on.

RANK AND FILE

On deck the fog breathed everywhere. He felt a dull pain in his side that mounted as a wave mounts, then quickly subsides. He distracted himself by playing a game of assessing the value of his organs, all that would be gone. For it occurred to him earlier, as the Captain made a dangerous pass close to a reef, that he wished to be cremated. The first bit of ash poured into a matchbox and entrusted to another damned young man, a sailor slipping it without ceremony into the inner pocket of his coat.

Pictures, an entire inventory, filed, offering salute:

An oversized *Gitane* with dancers in silhouette.

Blue, black, yellow.

Coarse hands.

A scarred dresser.

A cluster of grapes.

A fleet of ice. A torso rising.

Small hands sifting through black soil.

Small hands arranging soldiers on a shelf.

The fog seemed to glow and was everywhere save where he stood. He played another game of moving swiftly so as to observe the bright hole where he had been, but it moved with him—and the fluttering within was ominous and strange.

And he was transported to the October of his youth. The brilliant trees burned through the heavy mist and he climbed them to pluck leaves of gold, cramming fistfuls inside his sweater, imagining the wealth that would be his. But, in his own room, they had lost the properties contained in that eerie light and they were no longer gold. Just dry crinkling leaves. And he lay back on his pillow and stared up at the ceiling fathoming roses and serpents, surrendering upon a bed of leaves into the good graces of sleep.

The fog was lifting. The sea was exceptionally green.

Bells sounded . . . how he wished to shut them out.

Beneath closed eyes images, routes crisscrossed.

How he longed . . .

MUSIC (A WOMAN)

On deck a gentleman entertained a handful of guests in formal dress. Classical guitar studies, charming though a bit tedious. M kept at a distance and bowed his head, allowing himself to be drawn into the abstract monotony. The notes seemed to suspend and draw out in length, stroking the sea and himself. He began to nod at the rail but he did not wish to return to his cabin.

He found himself in the corridor of an unexplored section of the ship. He had wandered below, seduced by the scent of a familiar aria. He stood for a moment before a white enamel door, then slid to a crouching position to listen. After a time he was carried away, the strains of music tightening around him, forming a cocoon within which he dropped into sleep.

A woman opening the heavy door and another reality. "Here is where you ought to be tonight," the aria breathed, parting her garment. And he was enveloped once more.

Later he could hardly stand. He felt slightly numb and his legs had stiffened.

There was a singing in his skull. He felt the victim of some mischievous transformation. He pressed the wide curving walls for support and was relieved to reenter his cabin. He failed to notice a dress boot on its side but was amazed to find, on the center of his cot, a jewelled minaudiere which he hastily unclasped.

STAFF OF LIFE

He fell asleep and dreamed that Uncle was calling him. This disturbed him and made him feel uncomfortable about his uncle's belongings. He meditated a while on the word belonging and filled with immeasurable agitation gathered all the things he had brought aboard. He laid them carefully in Uncle's duffle, resolving to toss it over the side. But upon reexamining the bag itself he regretted his decision. It was so lovely, of worn ostrich skin, like parchment that had been brushed for centuries by a singular wind. The clasps and locks were cast in Chinese gold, pure and soft with a powdery texture. How many times had he watched with great anticipation Uncle opening this same bag and extracting from it some marvelous souvenir. M sat on the cot and held it fast as if he were a child clutching a cherished toy. He held it close and fell back, lulled by the old and feral sea . . .

He had been his uncle's favorite and sole heir. Knowing this he had often found himself dreaming of the bounty that would one day be his. And although he adored his uncle he could not resist turning precious objects in his hand and inhaling with secret pride all the intoxicating scents of Uncle's grounds. The stables,

the garden, the Chinese vases, the rows of first editions and his uncle's jewel cases. He was shocked at the zest with which he catalogued the estate, even when the time came, in the center of his overwhelming grief.

He dreamed. He slept. He did not dream at all. Rather he was overcome by an estranged sense of love. An apron of eyes that shook and popped like so many bulbs. And then nothing. Nothing in the garden that extended to the sea. Save one bloom from one such bulb. A singular tulip. Long, lone and black as a spot on the sun.

AFTER THOUGHTS

The bells sounded. An invitation to dine with the Captain had arrived by hand. He had no desire to attend save for the pleasure of laying out his best shirts. He could no longer eat; solids passed through him with the violence of a cloud. He drew his nourishment from a banquet of eyes. He dined on desire. And he was desired, courted yet most unyielding. For he was becoming indifferent, cold as if shot by marble. And marble guarded possessively whom it had entered. The untried veins, the slope of shoulders. He was aware of the swirling agitation in which he was the center, expelling it all in an irregular breath, in a twisted sigh.

To walk upon the mists beguiled . . .

His mother, suppressing a cry, watched him depart. Her boy. She longed to stop him, but something kept her. The love she felt was indistinct, yet present, gently prodding, pushing him on. He didn't want to go. He knew the marsh was dangerous. He knew as well that nothing could harm him, not now. It was not his time, and he would know, to the very moment, but not then and not at this moment as he laid his shirts across the cot.

He had walked across the marsh and he was ready. How should he achieve his goal. He would comb the ancient mangrove swamps, dive headlong into the healing pools formed by gods and crawl dry in jungle alive with orchids. He would dine on pollen. He would adorn himself with orchid rouge.

He rejected several shirts. Their material, extremely fine, seemed coarse and his every nerve was aflame. He recalled his burning feet, as he raced across a black beach, and an encounter with a youth, lying naked across the lush grasses. Black sand, red skin, acid lawn and perfect sky. He found the shirt he was looking for, of a material spun of silk and muscle, light, breathable and becoming.

How would he achieve his goal. The heat was abominable. There was fear of malaria, but fever was his brother; it pumped his marble veins with fire. Nights shuddering and wrapped in sheeting soaked in the tears shed from every pore.

The carriage would whisk him away quite early . . .

Through the mists, beguiled . . .

How would he achieve his goal. He would simply enter the scene, draped in muslin, his dark locks adorned with Dutchman's-pipe, and grasp what was to be his. He would spirit time and enter, then emerge unscathed. An angel falling and reclaiming mobility. The natives were children. He would surely be canonized. And his movement among them a frail eternal wind. Boys would rise as men, netting great uncommon wings to release in his memory and to expire exhausted upon the wave near the restless rocks in the cradle where Morpheus sleeps.

The bells sounded. He was ready and the table laid. He was, in the flickering light, quite beautiful. So much so as to make the Captain quite uncomfortable. As M anticipated, he was not able to dine, but this uneasiness on the part of his host was fare enough. He would take nothing save a clear broth and some port which would settle his stomach and allow him to be merry. As the evening heightened, wisdom blushed and he found himself trailing off from the intimate swirl of laughter and claret into the interior of a gravure above the Captain's desk. A woman, with her hair piled high, lifting her long skirt as she stepped into the high grass, gently pressing the shoulder of a small boy reaching for the velvet wing of a mourning cloak.

AN AUCTIONED HEART

The image of a girl in a lace cap with wings. A miraculous servant or Sister Mercury. Her profile, her gestures once elusive now expanding in perfect miniature. He called for tea which was a long time in coming. He laid back and thought of his uncle's house and the drawing room washed in violent light. In the garden, a girl with an umbrella turning. He felt a bit ill and the tea was tepid. He pressed the damp bags against his closed lids and fell into a series of stills, a pale orchid crushed by a hand paler still, a girl without a jewel offering her naked neck. Desire, a liquid, trickling her throat, her breast, sliding her open knees. He stood in the wilting shadow. Her weeping filled him with revulsion mixed with love. A love that only Cupid in mischievous sleep could muster. And only M in cruel awakening could master.

A BED OF ROSES

He had come to the conclusion that each of us knows everything, for destiny is our familiar, she permeates our breath. Hers is the atmosphere whereon a babe pillows his head. Signs wave their arms as we pass over. Lovers avert their eyes until the quivering recognition becomes unbearable, and they part. Each holding a piece of future fitting together like a dime-store heart.

He was destined to be ill, and part of him knew it. But he did not wish to address it, not now. So he fled into the bowels of tedium disguised as adventure— a liner in the center of the sea; into a mind untapped—pure and roomy. Here time stretched like a superhero of elastic clay. Here destiny could be courted and swept off her feet. Such a prospect filled him with tremendous resolve and he grasped the signs, molding and remolding them.

He leaned against the rail, euphoric, drumming scores of tiny thorns into the sea. And there he surrendered—a youth spread-eagle upon a bed of roses. A burning held like a claw within his swelling belly, which he slit with his own hand—too numb to feel, too ecstatic to speak.

MONKEYSHINES

He was freezing within and thawing without and the process would reverse. His being was at odds with his being; he sought the thing that would make him whole. He would capture his specimen and tack it to his person using the dotted pins he had secured from a botanist in London. Its properties would become his own through the prayers and rituals he had gathered.

He opened his clenched fist. He was crushing a large pearl. It was a true pearl, taking on his heat and emitting an ominous sickly glow. It had been a gift; how he had admired it. But upon examining it, he felt nothing and had the impulse to let it drop in the white water. A fleeting image of the giver filled him with unexpected nostalgia and he slid it into his vest pocket and let himself slide as well.

And he dipped in the very pool he sought to escape. And wading in rags was first love with all its ridiculous gestures. In the shallow water, a girl, bending over an expired turtle wrapped in eyelet lace, expressing all her sorrow in a possessed and angular dance.

He saw in her movements the movements of another. An exotic little fellow his uncle smuggled from India. The creature was not able to adapt fully and died in his little pen in the corner of the drawing room. Reacting with curiosity, M had boiled the head clean in an earthenware pot and came to cherish the small skull. Polishing it with chamois he saw it become his discreet companion, trusted with all his youthful soliloquies. He smiled at the thought, but quite unexpectedly one of the funny motions of the little fellow came to him, all his vibrant life. And he felt the shock of absence, even a bit of remorse. For he knew he had grown to love the skull more than the spirit that had given it life.

And now, as his own was fading, he wished to grasp that funny little spirit once more and engulf himself in the rapture of its play.

The diary of his thoughts spun as fine as veins of carnival glass. And in the center was a small oval portrait of a young man, filled with reproach, slightly out of focus, with a button missing from his coat and the threads tangled like rebellious strands of hair.

And leaves of a calendar flitted by. One such sheet cut into an exposed wrist. 22 May 1885, Victor Hugo dies. The route of his life's work hung with black crepe. It was said he used others but none so much as he used himself.

The clouds were shifting mischievously. He was jolted from his reverie and gazed upon them. Beyond them streaks of night were approaching. A young girl's mantle composed of ribbons of black crepe that disintegrated in a reign of tears.

THE HERCULEAN MOTH

Obscured by a love of his own design he withdrew, like Queequeg, within himself, making ready for the final stage of this love, powerful as it was . . .

He was departing from where he belonged. Or rather, where he arranged his belongings. All the rare and lovely trappings traded for the remote and wild. Wild as the hair of the Baptist. He laughed aloud at this notion and took pleasure in looking back upon small hands turning the leaves of the Book of Life. For there among the renderings of the pious and the civilized was the beloved barbarian, the cry in the wilderness, who dined on prayers and locusts. How the image of that cry repelled and fascinated him. He was moved by this little memory. For he had quite forgotten the hours spent contemplating that possessed, solitary figure.

He was himself suffering a transfiguration, a calling for which he would sacrifice his own head; set it upon a plate, without whimper or regret. For he desired nothing more than to release his own soul so that it might pierce the throne like a bullet or crawl upon the cloth like a babe.

He reached for the volume he had brought aboard, an insect file of the Southern

Hemisphere. He removed his coat, a walking coat of spun green velvet. Leafing through the volume he noted a worn spot in the sleeve. And how it seemed to shimmer like the worn skin of a wing. Now he turned his attention to the book in his hand—colored plates captioned with black letters. He sought his deliverer, the great bird wing of Papua, but another image captured his eye.

Coscincera Hercules. Wingspan 35 centimeters. There was his champion! Not a butterfly at all, though extraordinary. The Herculean Moth. So as to take on the strength of the ages. Become what he was not. A god physical; a muscular principle paving the night. He extracted a blade from his wallet, carefully removed the plate and divided it into four sections.

He covered his shoulders with his uncle's throw and hastened above. The sky was black and glistening as if spread with fresh tar. Points burning through the blackness produced the Southern Cross. His stare pierced these points, tiny arrows burning with the seductive poison of love. The Southern Cross. A sign lavished upon an inspired heaven. A sign of eyes, lips, eternal stamina. He reached into the night, fastening a wing, an antenna, and another wing as an offering, murmuring, "My darling, my precious myth, my god . . ."

The Herculean Moth, as iron as dresses. Bowing his head he felt something brush his cheek. It was his own lash which he removed with the delicate touch of a collector.

THE SOLOMON ISLANDS

Did they harbor something wise, a discreet combination of the vicious and the beautiful . . . Dead fish. Birds that whistled like ecstatic kettles. Drums, desire.

Was he a brief flash, a gleaming edge . . . Was he the sword, the instrument of a god or deluded and truly alone . . .

The petals, bright as a cheek, fell about him, dusting his hair. The crown jewels of Morpheus. So a god chooses after all, he whispered, and I am relieved and I renew my vows. He reviewed the particulars of his final act, and each phase fell as the petals shaking from his locks.

A sharp bit of wind caught the hem of the throw. It was not the warrior, nor the war, but certain rituals and relics of war that he adored. The scarf of the samurai, the bowl of sake spilled into the divine wind. And as he examined the cut and tone of his own tokens he achieved the demeanor of one who belonged to no one, nothing, save his dream, his destiny. And to this he was a slave.

THE PEDESTAL

"Life being more than all to me . . ."
W. H. Hudson

The spiritual sea was the sea of Turner. Heavy mists punctuated with cold capricious light. He had not slept. He sought comfort in a cigarette, in the feel of a delicately hammered match case and the containment in the moving scroll—the changing sea beyond the porthole. He sat for a while on the edge of the cot and opened a small crimson book that had been a favorite of his uncle. It was heavily underscored and one line in particular pierced him through, producing the unexpected shock of heartache.

He rose and disrobed. He stood before the long glass, and dressed slowly, deliberately, as if for a match, in linen fine as winding cloth. He took several deep breaths, for his heart, deeply fueled by his assertive action, was beating madly. He turned and surveyed the cabin. The ebony bootjack, a translucent pitcher and bowl, his drafting instruments and the cobalt inkwell wherein he had capped so many demons. Nothing jarred, all was as he wished, and saluting with a glance he exited and fairly marched, from level to level, until he reached the promenade, which was desolate.

He longed, for an instant, to take hold of one small waist and waltz upon the highly polished boards. To charm beauty, to be bold and seductive, to be intoxicated by love; a reason to believe.

A knot upon the stair.

Liberation, dear lady, free as I am. They circled. Liberated by what, by whom? By wind, by the whims of a magnificent statue? It couldn't matter. Thus free how shall I be cast—springing from the poised forefinger of a young girl, or from a pedestal skyrocketing, spewing hard bits of marble into the angry mists? He inhaled the unholy sea, for so it now seemed. The deafening foghorn was a great lily heralding him away.

What cord would bind him? A waft of music? A ribbon raving? How should he be decorated? A pair of clever wings fashioned in gold, an ancient garment, or the remnants of a child's coat dissolving in a vat of tears?

He steadied himself. He had in welcomed such lamenting for he was feverish and the tears of the adoring cooled him until he became powerless to stop their flow. Such tears filled him with revulsion. No one could enter a soul composed of tears, for one would surely drown.

He stood exactly where he stood at the onset of his voyage. And it occurred to him, at this place, having no heir, no beloved, that he was alone. And he must be to himself his own son and his own father and his own companion. To love and to elevate oneself as a god pressing against the blue and burning into form.

And all at once the beauteous complexity of the self in its purity and its vanity was revealed to him, burning into a form of its own, a form of knowledge luxuriant as a forest untouched save by the miraculous frivolity of nature.

And the sea turned about him. A being given to the sea amidst sighs of release. And for a brief moment he mourned the wave and luster of his own hair; of a precious head of curls once treasured by a mother. Curls that would flow straight in the layers of the deep until, the cycle complete, he would be free, the crux of his own desire.

The sleeves of his white shirt billowed. He addressed the foam. Purity, in the arms of a child, is a smothered lamb, a crushed joy.

For one great moment he saw the foam mount and mushroom, a torso of cloud that hardened, a pedestal composed of the elements. And he opened his shirt for he desired nothing more than to stretch across and be absorbed.

And his blood was sounding and his ears were ringing and he was disconcerted and more than a little annoyed to find that he was weeping.

LITANY

CRUX

"What is the point?" he cried out. "What is the point?"

And the heavy mists, a confusion of salt, drew about him, embracing him as a spider embraces his prey. And he could feel, in the center of his being, another being, praying for him to no avail. For he was party to a delicious submission, evil, full of love, far from a mortal's reach and a mortal's cup.

And he saw a small boy plucking the points from the southern sky and dropping them into a silver urn. He saw a river of leaves and the boy bending to brush the leaves from his shoes. And he was suddenly aware of tears falling and staining his own shoes.

"What is the point?" he whispered. "What is the point?"

And he removed his shirt. And he felt immeasurably free. And the heavy mists drew about him, filling him until he seemed to run over with a thrill of recognition.

"You sir, you are the point."

MAGUA

And he spread his naked arms to the sun like a savage. Stretched them into dawn, into warmth. And he believed he could adapt to anything. His elevated temperature would gift him with unlimited mobility. Then nourished, refreshed he would harden, expand.

And all the muscles were contracting.

And he could feel it coming and all he could do was draw what he could and shed what was wretched.

And all the muscles were contracting.

And images rushed with Amazon force. Some pleasurable, some liquid. A glowing hive, a helmet of skin. And he could feel everything. The purity wherein all formulas of light and death are exposed.

And all the muscles were contracting.

And he was emerging, drenched and pink and vibrant, the skin pulled back by the hand of God.

IMAGO

And abruptly, as though wrenched, reason was forced to break forth in the form of a Herculean span prevailing over the sky like a victory sign. The spectacle, golden, monstrous, burned through a curtain of lids; of certain eyes. And the Captain, on the foredeck, marveled, as did the first mate.

For M had departed the hold of the Coral Sea and invested destiny by fixing his great wings upon her bosom, commending these same wings beneath the folding arms of the deaconess of his soul.

The author wishes to thank the Estate of Robert Mapplethorpe,

Michael Alago, Amy Cherry, Janet Hamill,

Edward Maxey, and Oliver Ray.

LIST OF ILLUSTRATIONS

Photographs by Robert Mapplethorpe: p. 7: Photo booth picture courtesy of Patti Smith; p. 18: *The Coral Sea* (1983); p. 27: *New Orleans Interior* (1982); p. 29: *Statue Series* (1983); p. 34: *Pear* (1985); p. 37: *Stems* (1985); p. 42: *Sleeping Cupid* (1989); p. 47: *Rose* (1977); p. 51: *The Sluggard* (1988); p. 54: *Whiting & Co. Water Pitcher* (1988); p. 62: *Ganymede/Eagle* (1988); p. 65: *Orchid with Hand* (1983); p. 69: *Lake Mephramagog* (1979); p. 71: *Patti Smith* (1987). Copyright © The Estate of Robert Mapplethorpe. Used by permission. All rights reserved.

Photograph by Lynn Davis: pp. 58 and 59: *Disko Bay, Jakobshaven, Greenland* (1988). © Lynn Davis 1988. Reproduced by permission.

Photograph by Edward Maxey: p. 4: *Hol Chan, Belize* (1992). © Edward Maxey. Reproduced by permission.